Health

Family
Favourites

C000065878

KÖNEMANN

Favourite Family Menus

Whether it's a family celebration dinner, a casual buffet or relaxed barbecue in the garden, there's a menu here which will be perfect for the occasion.

Barbecue for 10

EGGPLANT DIP

VEGIE BURGERS

TANGY COLESLAW

SPICY CHICKEN KEBABS

TOMATO SALAD

CORN MUFFINS

FROZEN PEACH ICE

Eggplant Dip

Preparation time:
  15 minutes
Total cooking time:
  30 minutes
Makes 4 cups

3 large eggplant
1 clove garlic,
  crushed
*1/3 cup tahini (sesame
  paste)*
1/4 cup lemon juice

1 Preheat oven to moderate 180°C. Line an oven tray with aluminium foil. Cut eggplant in half lengthways; place cut-side down on prepared tray. Bake 30 minutes or until very soft. Remove from oven; cool.

2 Scrape eggplant flesh from the skin. Place in food processor bowl with garlic, tahini and juice. Using pulse action, press button 1 minute or until just smooth.

3 Transfer eggplant mixture to a serving bowl. Cover and refrigerate until required. Allow to come to room temperature before serving. Serve with fresh vegetables, such as carrot sticks, celery sticks, slices of cucumber, asparagus or tiny radishes.

Eggplant Dip (left) and Vegie Burgers (page 4).

Vegie Burgers

Preparation time:
  30 minutes +
  overnight soaking
Total cooking time:
  1 hour 8 minutes + 30
  minutes refrigeration
Makes 10

2 cups dried chickpeas
1/2 teaspoon olive oil
1 medium onion, very
  finely chopped
2 medium zucchini,
  grated
1 large carrot,
  grated
1/2 cup fresh wholemeal
  breadcrumbs
1/2 teaspoon sweet
  paprika
1/2 teaspoon ground
  oregano
freshly ground black
  pepper
2 egg whites, lightly
  beaten

1 Cover chickpeas with
cold water, soak
overnight. Drain, wash
well and cover with
fresh water. Cook in a
large pan, over low
heat, for 1 hour.
2 Heat oil in frying
pan. Stir-fry onion,
zucchini and carrot
until soft. Transfer to a
large mixing bowl to
cool. Drain chickpeas
and mash with a potato
masher until broken up.
Add to vegetables with
breadcrumbs, paprika,
oregano and pepper.

Mix together until well
combined; stir in egg
whites.
3 Using hands, form
mixture into 10 equal
patties. Place on tray.
Cover with plastic
wrap. Refrigerate for
30 minutes before
cooking. Place burgers
on a lightly greased
barbecue or flat plate;
cook for 3-4 minutes
each side or until
golden. Serve with Thai
sweet chilli sauce.

Tangy Coleslaw

Preparation time:
  20 minutes
Total cooking time:
  Nil
Serves 10

350 g white cabbage,
  finely shredded
200 g red cabbage,
  finely shredded
1 large carrot, grated
2 spring onions, finely
  sliced
1/4 cup apple juice
1 tablespoon cider
  vinegar
1/2 teaspoon French
  mustard

1 Place cabbage, carrot
and onion in a large
serving bowl. Use
hands to combine
thoroughly.
2 Place remaining
ingredients in a small
jar. Shake vigorously
for 30 seconds or until

combined. Pour over
vegetables and toss
lightly to combine.
Serve immediately.

Note: Vegetables may
be prepared and
refrigerated until
required. Dress
coleslaw just before
serving to keep
vegetables crisp.

Spicy Chicken Kebabs

Preparation time:
  15 minutes +
  2 hours marinating
Total cooking time:
  12 minutes
Makes 10 kebabs

1 kg chicken
  tenderloins
3/4 cup plain low-fat
  yoghurt
2 tablespoons finely
  chopped coriander
1/2 teaspoon ground
  cumin
1/2 teaspoon ground
  coriander
2 teaspoons finely
  grated ginger
1 tablespoon curry
  powder

1 Trim meat of excess
fat and sinew. Cut
tenderloins in half;
place in a shallow
non-metal dish.
2 Combine remaining
ingredients and spread
over chicken. Store,
covered, in refrigerator

Tangy Coleslaw (top) and Spicy Chicken Kebabs.

for 2 hours, turning occasionally.
3 Drain meat and thread onto bamboo skewers. Place on a preheated, lightly greased barbecue grill or flat plate. Cook for 6 minutes each side. Serve immediately.

Note: Chicken breast fillets may be substituted for the tenderloins in this recipe if desired. Trim the breasts of all fat and sinew and cut them into strips about 2 cm wide and 5 cm long.

HINT
To avoid burning bamboo skewers on the barbecue or under the grill, soak them in water for at least one hour before threading meat onto them.

Tomato Salad.

Tomato Salad

Preparation time:
  10 minutes +
  1 hour refrigeration
Total cooking time:
  Nil
Serves 10

5 large ripe tomatoes
2 medium red
  onions
1 medium Lebanese
  cucumber

1–2 tablespoons
  balsamic vinegar
1/3 cup basil leaves

1 Cut tomatoes into
3 cm cubes. Peel onions
and slice thinly. Cut
cucumber into 2 cm
cubes. Place in bowl.
2 Sprinkle balsamic
vinegar over salad. Toss
lightly to combine and
refrigerate for at least
one hour. Remove from
refrigerator and allow
to come to room
temperature. Shred
basil finely; toss
through salad and serve
immediately.

Note: Balsamic vinegar
is an aged vinegar with
a unique flavour, from
delicatessens and some
supermarkets.

HINT
For tomatoes with a
full flavour, look for
those marked 'vine-
ripened'.

Corn Muffins.

Corn Muffins

Preparation time:
 15 minutes
Total cooking time:
 20 minutes
Makes 10

1¹/2 cups wholemeal
 flour
1 cup cornmeal
 (polenta)
1 teaspoon baking
 powder

¹/2 cup sun-dried
 tomatoes
1¹/4 cups buttermilk
2 tablespoons
 sunflower oil
1 egg, lightly beaten

1 Preheat oven to
moderate 180°C. Sift
flour, cornmeal and
baking powder into a
large mixing bowl;
place husks in bowl.
Add sun-dried
tomatoes.
2 Place buttermilk, oil

and egg into a jug;
whisk until well
combined. Make a well
in centre of dry
ingredients; add milk
mixture and stir with a
wooden spoon until
just combined.
3 Divide mixture
between 10 cups of a
non-stick muffin tin.
Bake for 20 minutes.
Allow to cool in tin for
5 minutes before
carefully lifting them
out. Serve warm.

7

Frozen Peach Ice

Preparation time:
  20 minutes +
  4 hours freezing
Total cooking time:
  Nil
Serves 10

2 x 825 g cans peach
  slices in natural juice
2 teaspoons
  honey
2 teaspoons vanilla
  essence
1¹/2 teaspoons ground
  ginger

1 Place one can of peaches and the honey, vanilla and ginger in food processor bowl. Using pulse action, press button for 30 seconds or until mixture is smooth. Pour into a large mixing bowl. Process remaining peaches and add to first mixture; stir to combine.
2 Divide mixture between two 20 cm deep, round cake tins.

Cover with plastic wrap and freeze for 2 hours, until almost solid. Working on one tin at a time, place mixture in large mixing bowl. Beat with electric beaters for 1 minute to break up large ice crystals. Return mixture to tin. Repeat with remaining mixture. Cover with plastic wrap and return to freezer for 2 hours. Repeat beating process. Refreeze until just firm. Remove from freezer 5 minutes before serving. To serve, place mixture in parfait glasses and accompany with a selection of fresh fruit.

HINT
Almost any fruit can be used instead of peaches. Fresh fruit and fruit juice can be substituted for canned fruit. Use a combination of fruit and juice to make up the gram weight required.

Frozen Peach Ice.

Celebration Dinner for 6

MUSHROOM PÂTÉ
SWEET POTATO SOUP
RATATOUILLE
HERB ROAST LAMB
POTATO AND ONION CRISPS
STRAWBERRY MOUSSE

Mushroom Pâté

Preparation time:
  20 minutes
Total cooking time:
  15 minutes +
  1 hour refrigeration
Serves 6

2 teaspoons sunflower oil
1 small onion, finely chopped
1 clove garlic, crushed
1/4 cup white wine
700 g button mushrooms, thinly sliced
1/2 teaspoon dried thyme
1/3 cup ricotta cheese
black pepper to taste

1 Heat oil in a large pan. Stir-fry onion and garlic over medium heat until soft; add white wine, mushrooms and thyme. Cook, stirring occasionally, for 5 minutes or until very soft.
2 Reduce heat; cook 10 minutes more or until liquid has evaporated. Cool.

3 Place mushroom mixture, ricotta and pepper into food processor bowl. Using pulse action, press button 1 minute or until almost smooth. Line a 3-cup capacity deep bowl with plastic wrap, and spoon mixture into bowl. Press in firmly with the back of a spoon. Cover with plastic wrap and refrigerate for 1 hour, or spoon mixture into individual serving bowls and refrigerate until set. To serve, turn out onto a plate and serve with crackers or melba toast.

Mushroom Pâté (left) and Sweet Potato Soup (page 12).

Sweet Potato Soup

Preparation time:
  20 minutes
Total cooking time:
  25 minutes
Serves 6

1 teaspoon sunflower oil
2 large leeks, thinly
  sliced
1/2 teaspoon finely
  grated ginger
750 g sweet potato, cut
  into 3 cm cubes
1 teaspoon curry
  powder
1 litre water
yoghurt and chopped
  chives, to serve

1 Heat oil in a large
pan. Stir-fry leeks over
medium heat until soft.
Add ginger and cook a
further 2 minutes.
2 Add sweet potato
and cover with water.
Bring to the boil;
reduce heat and simmer,
covered, 20 minutes,
stirring occasionally.
Remove from heat. Cool.
3 Using a blender or
food processor, blend
soup in batches until
smooth. Return to pan
and reheat to serve.
Serve with a dollop of
yoghurt. Sprinkle with
chopped chives.

Ratatouille

Preparation time:
  20 minutes
Total cooking time:
  25 minutes
Serves 6

1 teaspoon olive oil
1 large onion, chopped
2 cloves garlic, crushed
3 slender eggplant
3 medium zucchini
1 medium red capsicum
1 medium green
  capsicum
2 large tomatoes
1 teaspoon dried basil

1 Heat oil in a large
pan. Stir-fry onion and
garlic until soft. Cut
eggplant and zucchini
into 2 cm slices; cut
capsicum into 2 cm
squares. Add zucchini
and capsicum to onion
and stir-fry 3 minutes,
until just soft.
2 Cut tomatoes into
3 cm cubes and add to
vegetable mixture with
basil. Cover and cook
over low heat for
15 minutes, stirring
occasionally.
3 Uncover pan; cook a
further 5 minutes,
stirring occasionally,
until some of the liquid
has evaporated.
Serve immediately.

Herb Roast Lamb

Preparation time:
  30 minutes
Total cooking time:
  45 minutes
Serves 6

2 x 500 g boned lean
  lamb loins
1/2 cup parsley, large
  stalks removed
1/4 cup basil leaves
1/4 cup mint leaves
1 tablespoon chopped
  chives
2 cloves garlic, crushed
2 teaspoons olive oil
freshly ground black
  pepper, to taste
2 teaspoons oil, extra

1 Preheat oven to
moderate 180°C. Trim
meat of excess fat and
sinew. Place herbs,
garlic and oil in
processor bowl. Using
pulse action, press
button for 20 seconds
or until mixture is
almost smooth.
2 Lay meat out flat.
Spread each loin with
herb mixture, roll up.
Tie with string at
intervals to keep shape.
3 Place meat on rack in
a large baking dish.
Brush with extra oil.
Sprinkle with black
pepper. Bake 45 minutes.
Remove from oven and
leave, covered with foil,
in a warm place for
5 minutes. Remove
string before slicing.

From top: Ratatouille, Herb Roast Lamb and Potato and Onion Crisps.

Potato and Onion Crisps

Preparation time:
20 minutes
Total cooking time:
30 minutes
Serves 6

6 *small potatoes*
1 *small onion*

2 *teaspoons olive*
  oil
1/4 *teaspoon French*
  mustard
2 *teaspoons orange*
  rind

1 Preheat oven to moderate 180°C. Peel potatoes and slice very finely. Peel and slice onion very finely. Combine potatoes and

onions in a large mixing bowl.
2 Combine oil, mustard and rind. Add to the potato mixture. Using hands, toss thoroughly to combine. Spread potatoes onto a non-stick baking tray or pizza tray. Bake for 30 minutes or until golden. Serve immediately.

13

For *Strawberry Mousse:* Add gelatine to blended strawberries, yoghurt and honey.

Beat egg whites in a small bowl until soft peaks form.

Strawberry Mousse

Preparation time:
  35 minutes
Total cooking time:
  30 minutes +
  2 hours refrigeration
Serves 6

250 g punnet
  strawberries
2 cups low-fat
  strawberry yoghurt
2 teaspoons honey
1 tablespoon gelatine
2 tablespoons
  water
250 g punnet
  strawberries, extra

Meringues
1 egg white
¼ cup sugar

1 Lightly brush a 2-cup capacity ring or decorative mould with oil.
2 Place strawberries, yoghurt and honey in food processor bowl. Using pulse action, press button for 30 seconds or until smooth.
3 Combine gelatine with water in a small bowl. Stand bowl in boiling water; stir until dissolved. Add to yoghurt mixture. Process further 5 seconds until combined. Pour into prepared tin and refrigerate 2 hours, or until set.
4 To make Meringues: Preheat oven to slow 150°C. Brush an oven tray with oil. Line with baking paper. Place egg white in a small dry mixing bowl. Using electric beaters, beat egg whites until soft peaks form. Add sugar gradually, beating until mixture is thick and glossy and all the sugar is dissolved.
5 Spoon mixture into a piping bag fitted with a large fluted nozzle; pipe 18 small round meringues onto prepared tray. Bake for 30 minutes, until pale and crisp. Turn oven off. Cool meringues completely on tray in oven, with the door slightly ajar.
6 To serve, invert mousse carefully onto serving platter. Surround with some of the meringues, and extra strawberries. Serve the remaining meringues separately.

> **HINT**
> Instead of using strawberries, try other berries, such as raspberries, blueberries or blackberries, if they are available. Frozen berries can be purchased from the freezer section of most supermarkets.

Strawberry Mousse.

Spoon meringue mixture into piping bag; pipe rounds on prepared tray.

To serve, invert mousse onto serving platter; surround with meringues.

Spicy Buffet for 8

RED LENTIL DIP
BEEF CURRY
FRAGRANT VEGETABLES
CARROT AND POPPYSEED SALAD
CUCUMBER AND MELON SALAD
CINNAMON POACHED PEARS
WITH VANILLA YOGHURT

Red Lentil Dip

Preparation time:
  10 minutes
Total cooking time:
  25 minutes
Serves 8

1 1/4 cups red lentils
1 teaspoon olive oil
1 clove garlic, crushed
1 medium onion, finely
  chopped
1/2 teaspoon ground
  ginger
1 teaspoon turmeric
1 teaspoon garam
  masala
2 cups water

1 Place lentils in a
large bowl and cover
with water. Remove
any floating particles
and drain well. Heat oil
in a medium pan; stir-
fry garlic and onion
over low heat until soft.
Add ginger, turmeric
and garam masala and
stir-fry 1 minute more.
2 Add lentils and
water. Bring to the boil
and simmer for

15–20 minutes, stirring
occasionally. Be careful
that the mixture does
not stick and burn.
Transfer to a serving
bowl to cool. Serve
with toasted pitta bread.

Beef Curry

Preparation time:
  30 minutes
Total cooking time:
  1 hour 12 minutes
Serves 8

1.2 kg lean blade steak
1 tablespoon peanut oil
2 large onions, chopped
1 tablespoon grated
  ginger
3 cloves garlic, crushed
1 tablespoon ground
  coriander
2 teaspoons ground
  cumin
1/2 teaspoon ground
  black pepper
1 teaspoon chilli
  powder
3 x 425 g cans tomato
  purée
500 g pumpkin, cut
  into 2 cm cubes

Red Lentil Dip (top) and Beef Curry.

1 Trim meat of excess fat and sinew; cut into 3 cm cubes. Heat oil in a large heavy-based pan. Add onions, ginger and garlic, cook gently for 10 minutes or until onions are soft, stirring occasionally.
2 Add coriander, cumin, pepper and chilli powder; stir-fry for 2 minutes. Add tomato purée.
3 Add meat. Bring to the boil. Reduce heat and simmer, uncovered, for 45 minutes, stirring occasionally. Add the pumpkin and cook a further 15 minutes or until tender. Serve with boiled white rice and pappadums.

Note: Some brands of pappadum can be cooked in the microwave on a paper towel.

Fragrant Vegetables

Preparation time:
 30 minutes
Total cooking time:
 35 minutes
Serves 8

1 tablespoon olive oil
1 large onion, finely chopped
2 cloves garlic, crushed
1 cinnamon stick
1 teaspoon chopped fresh chilli

2 teaspoons ground coriander
2 teaspoons ground cumin
200 g (1 medium) eggplant, cut into 2 cm cubes
3 medium carrots, sliced
150 g sweet potato, cut into 1 cm cubes
400 g can chickpeas
100 g green beans, cut into 3 cm lengths
2 zucchini, cut into 2 cm cubes
1/2 cup boiling water
1 large tomato, chopped
1 tablespoon chopped parsley
1 tablespoon chopped coriander

1 Heat oil in a large pan; add onion, garlic and cinnamon stick and cook for 2 minutes, until onion is soft. Add chilli, coriander, cumin, eggplant, carrots and sweet potato. Cover; cook over a low heat for 10 minutes, stirring occasionally.
2 Add chickpeas, beans, zucchini and water; stir to combine. Bring to boil, reduce heat and simmer, covered, 15 minutes. Add tomato and cook uncovered a further 5 minutes. Stir in herbs and serve with rice.

Cucumber and Melon Salad

Preparation time:
 15 minutes
Total cooking time:
 Nil
Serves 8

1 medium rockmelon (cantaloupe)
2 Lebanese cucumbers
2 small red onions
1 tablespoon chopped parsley

1 Cut rockmelon in half. Scoop out seeds, peel and cut flesh into 1 cm cubes. Repeat with cucumbers, leaving skin on. Place in a serving bowl.
2 Chop onions finely, and add to bowl with parsley. Toss well to combine. Cover and refrigerate for 1 hour before serving.

Cucumber and Melon Salad (top) and Fragrant Vegetables.

Carrot and Poppyseed Salad

Preparation time:
  15 minutes
Total cooking time:
  Nil
Serves 8

3 large carrots
1/2 cup sultanas
1 tablespoon
  poppyseeds
1 tablespoon lemon
  juice
1 tablespoon orange
  juice
2 teaspoons honey

1 Finely grate carrots, place into a serving bowl. Add sultanas and poppyseeds, toss to combine.
2 Combine juices and honey, pour over carrots. Stir until carrots are coated in dressing. Cover and refrigerate until required.

Cinnamon Pears with Vanilla Cream

Preparation time:
  20 minutes
Total cooking time:
  20 minutes
Serves 8

3 cups natural pear or
  apple juice
2 cups water
8 medium pears
3 cinnamon sticks
2 tablespoons sherry

Vanilla Cream
3/4 cup reduced-fat
  yoghurt
1/2 teaspoon vanilla
  essence
2 teaspooons honey

1. Place juice and water in pan; bring to boil. Peel pears, leaving stalks intact. Place in juice with cinnamon and sherry, return to boil. Reduce heat; simmer, covered, 20 minutes, turning occasionally. Do not overcook. Pears should retain shape. Remove from pan; cool at room temperature.
2. To make Vanilla Cream: Combine ingredients. Serve a pear on each plate with a dollop of Vanilla Cream.

Carrot and Poppyseed Salad (left) and Cinnamon Pears with Vanilla Cream.

Main Meals

Healthy food can be hearty and delicious, as well as nourishing. In this chapter are all the old favourites – roast lamb, fish and chips, pizza and lasagne, to name but a few. However, the cooking methods and ingredients have been modified to follow today's guidelines for healthy eating.

Sweet and Sour Chicken

Preparation time:
  45 minutes
Total cooking time:
  15 minutes
Serves 6

4 chicken breast fillets, skin removed
2 spring onions, roughly chopped
1 strip lemon rind
6 peppercorns

Sauce
1 teaspoon vegetable oil
2 teaspoons grated ginger
2 small onions, quartered
2 large carrots, thinly sliced
2 sticks of celery, sliced diagonally
1 small red capsicum, seeded, sliced

400 g can pineapple pieces in natural juice (drain, reserve 1 cup juice)
2 tablespoons brown vinegar
1 tablespoon salt-reduced soy sauce
1 tablespoon tomato paste, no added salt
1 teaspoon soft brown sugar
1 tablespoon lemon juice
3 teaspoons cornflour
1/4 cup chicken stock (recipe overleaf)
1 small cucumber, cut in half lengthways and sliced

1 Place chicken in medium pan and cover with cold water. Add lemon rind, spring onions and peppercorns. Bring slowly to the boil. Reduce heat; simmer, covered, for 6 minutes.

Sweet and Sour Chicken (top) and Vegetable Frittatas.

Remove chicken from stock. Reserve stock. Chill. Remove fat from surface of stock. Slice chicken; cover, keep warm.

2 To prepare sauce: Heat oil in medium pan. Add ginger and onion and cook over high heat 1 minute. Add carrot, celery and capsicum; cook, stirring, 2 minutes.

3 Add pineapple juice, vinegar, soy sauce, tomato paste, sugar and lemon juice; stir to combine. Blend chicken stock and cornflour; add and stir until mixture boils and thickens.

4 Add pineapple pieces, cucumber and chicken. Stir gently to combine. Serve with boiled or steamed rice.

Note: Any cooked chicken can be used but remember to remove all skin and fat.

HINT

To make chicken stock, put 250 g chicken bones in a pan, add 1 small chopped onion, $^1/_2$ small diced carrot, a few celery leaves, 2 peppercorns, a small bay leaf and 3 cups water. Simmer, uncovered, for 30 minutes, adding a little more water if necessary. Strain stock. Allow to cool completely, then remove any traces of fat from the surface.
Use as required. Leftover stock can be frozen if desired. Transfer to airtight container, seal, label and date. Freeze, using within eight weeks.

Vegetable Frittatas

Preparation time:
  15 minutes
Total cooking time:
  50 minutes
Serves 6

1 tablespoon
  polyunsaturated
  margarine
3 spring onions,
  chopped
2 zucchini, sliced
100 g mushrooms,
  sliced
1 medium red
  capsicum, chopped
160 g can corn kernels
4 eggs, lightly beaten
$^1/_2$ cup low-fat yoghurt
1 tablespoon finely
  chopped basil

1 Preheat oven to moderate 180°C. Brush a 23 cm round quiche dish with a little melted margarine. Heat remaining margarine

in large frying pan; add spring onions and cook until golden. Add zucchini, mushrooms, capsicum and corn and cook over medium heat for further 5 minutes or until soft. Remove from heat. Drain off any excess liquid.

2 Combine eggs and yoghurt in large bowl; add vegetables and basil. Mix well.

3 Pour mixture into prepared quiche dish. Bake 40 minutes or until set. Cut into wedges. Serve hot, warm or cold with a green salad.

Beef Stir-fry

Preparation time:
  20 minutes
Total cooking time:
  15 minutes
Serves 4-6

500 g lean rump
  steak
1 tablespoon peanut oil
1 clove garlic,
  crushed
1 tablespoon grated
  fresh ginger
3 spring onions,
  diagonally sliced
2 carrots, sliced
1 zucchini,
  sliced
100 g mushrooms,
  sliced
100 g snow peas
1 tablespoon cornflour

Beef Stir-fry.

2 tablespoons
  water
1 tablespoon salt-
  reduced soy sauce
1 tablespoon sweet
  chilli sauce

1 Trim meat of excess fat and sinew. Cut into thin strips.
2 Heat oil in large frying pan or wok over medium heat. Add oil, garlic and spring onions. Cook over medium heat 3 minutes or until golden.
3 Add beef; stir-fry over high heat for 3 minutes or until browned. Add carrots, zucchini, mushrooms and snow peas and stir-fry for 3 minutes.
4 Combine cornflour, water, soy sauce and chilli sauce in small bowl. Add to pan and stir until smooth. Cook, stirring, until sauce boils and thickens. Serve with brown or white rice.

Quiche Lorraine

Preparation time:
  20 minutes
Total cooking time:
  40 minutes
Serves 6

4 sheets filo
  pastry
3 eggs, lightly
  beaten
1/2 cup yoghurt
80 g lean ham,
  sliced
2 spring onions,
  chopped
1 tablespoon finely
  chopped parsley
1/3 cup grated low-fat
  cheese

1 Preheat oven to moderate 180°C. Brush a 23 cm round quiche dish with melted margarine. Cut pastry sheets in half. Line quiche dish with pastry sheets. Cover with damp tea-towel to prevent pastry from drying out.
2 Combine eggs, yoghurt, ham, spring onions, parsley and cheese in large bowl. Mix well.
3 Pour egg mixture onto pastry base. Bake for 40 minutes or until set. Serve hot or cold, cut into wedges, with fresh salad greens.

Beef and Bean Burritos

Preparation time:
  20 minutes + 2 hours
  refrigeration
Total cooking time:
  20 minutes
Serves 4-6

1 tablespoon olive oil
1 medium onion,
  chopped
1 tablespoon ground
  cumin
1 tablespoon sweet
  paprika
1 tablespoon ground
  coriander
500 g lean beef mince
2 tablespoons mild taco
  sauce
440 g can red kidney
  beans, drained
12 lettuce leaves,
  shredded
3 tomatoes, sliced
  thinly
3 carrots, grated
1 avocado,
  sliced thinly
1/2 cup yoghurt
1/2 cup grated low-fat
  cheese
1 packet lavash bread

1 Heat oil in large non-stick frying pan. Add onion and cook over medium heat for 3–4 minutes or until golden. Add cumin, paprika and coriander; cook 2 minutes.
2 Add mince. Cook

5 minutes until well browned, using fork to break up any lumps as it cooks. Remove from heat. Spoon mince into bowl; cool. Cover with plastic wrap and refrigerate. Remove any excess fat with spoon and discard.
3 Heat mince in non-stick frying pan. Add taco sauce and kidney beans and cook over moderate heat for 5 minutes or until mixture thickens.
4 To serve, cut lavash bread in half crossways. Place 2-3 tablespoons of meat onto each piece of bread. Top with lettuce, tomato, carrot, avocado, a tablespoon of yoghurt, and sprinkle with cheese. Roll and serve hot or cold.

Note: Lavash bread may be replaced with wholemeal pitta bread or Lebanese bread. All these breads are available at the supermarket. Use lean pork or chicken mince in place of beef mince.

Beef and Bean Burritos (top) and Quiche Lorraine.

For Roast Lamb: Cover top of lamb with mint, lemon and garlic mixture.

Cut the unpeeled potatoes and pumpkin into even-sized pieces.

Roast Lamb with all the Trimmings

Preparation time:
  10 minutes
Total cooking time
  1 hour 45 minutes
Serves 6–8

1/4 cup fresh chopped
  mint
1 tablespoon olive oil
1 tablespoon lemon
  juice
2 teaspoons finely
  grated lemon rind
1 clove garlic, crushed
1.8 kg leg of lamb, all
  fat and sinew removed
8 medium new
  potatoes
16 pieces (1 kg)
  butternut pumpkin
1 tablespoon cornflour
1 1/4 cups chicken
  stock

1 Preheat oven to moderately slow 160°C. Combine mint, oil, lemon juice, rind and garlic in bowl. Place lamb on rack in a large baking dish. Fill baking dish to a depth of one-third with cold water. Cover top of lamb with mixture. Bake for 1 hour and 45 minutes or until the juices run clear when a skewer is placed in the thickest part of the meat.

2 Place unpeeled pieces of potato and pumpkin on rack in baking dish and start baking 50 minutes before lamb will be ready. Cook until well browned.

3 Remove lamb from oven and set aside. Pour away any water or fat remaining in dish. Blend cornflour and chicken stock, add to dish and stir about 3 minutes over low heat until gravy boils and thickens. Strain and keep warm.

4 Slice lamb; serve with potatoes, pumpkin and gravy, accompanied by steamed green beans and carrot sticks flavoured with freshly ground black pepper and lemon juice.

HINT
Ask the butcher to bone the leg of lamb for you. This will make it easier to carve. Lamb can be coated with mint mixture and allowed to marinate overnight in the refrigerator. This will intensify the flavour and tenderise the lamb.

Roast Lamb with all the Trimmings.

When gravy has boiled and thickened, strain and keep warm.

Slice lamb and serve with gravy, potatoes, pumpkin and other vegetables.

Fish and Chips

Preparation time:
  20 minutes
Total cooking time:
  30 minutes
Serves 4

6 potatoes, cut into
  thick wedges
2 tablespoons
  sunflower oil
4 (120 g each) perch
  fillets
1/2 cup plain flour
1 teaspoon ground
  cumin
1 teaspoon ground
  sweet paprika
2 egg whites, lightly
  beaten
2 cups cornflake crumbs

1 Preheat oven to
moderately hot 210°C
(190°C gas). Line two
oven trays with foil.
2 Brush potatoes with
oil; place on prepared
tray. Bake 30 minutes
or until crisp.
3 Pat dry fish fillets on
paper towel. Combine
flour, cumin and
paprika. Toss fish
lightly in seasoned
flour; shake off excess.
Dip fish into egg whites
one at a time. Coat

HINT
Use any white fish
fillets in this recipe.
Substitute fresh
breadcrumbs for
cornflake crumbs.

---

with crumbs, shake off
excess. Place on
prepared tray. Bake
for 15 minutes or until
fish flakes. Serve fish
and potato chips with a
mixed garden salad.

Tuna Casserole

Preparation time:
  30 minutes
Total cooking time:
  30 minutes
Serves 4–6

3/4 cup macaroni
  elbows
1 tablespoon canola oil
3 spring onions,
  chopped
2 leeks, thinly sliced
425 g can tuna, drained
  (no added salt)
160 g can corn
  kernels
1 tablespoon finely
  chopped thyme
1 tablespoon
  cornflour
1 1/2 cups low-fat milk

1/2 cup wholemeal
  breadcrumbs
2 tablespoons grated
  parmesan cheese

1 Preheat oven to
moderate 180°C. Cook
pasta in large pan of
rapidly boiling water
until just tender.
Drain, set aside.
2 Heat oil in large
frying pan. Add onions
and leek; cook over
moderate heat for
2 minutes or until
golden. Add tuna, corn
and thyme and cook
for 5 minutes.
3 Combine cornflour
and milk in small bowl
or jug, stir until
smooth. Add gradually
to pan, stirring over
medium heat 3 minutes
or until mixture boils
and thickens. Add
pasta; cook until
warmed through.
4 Spoon mixture
into 6-cup capacity
ovenproof dish.
Combine breadcrumbs
and cheese. Sprinkle
over pasta. Bake
20 minutes or until
golden. Serve hot with
fresh green salad and
crusty bread.

Note: To make
Macaroni Cheese,
replace the tuna with
one cup of grated low-
fat cheese. Use any
shape of pasta in
this recipe.

Tuna Casserole (top) and Fish and Chips.

Crisp Crumbed Chicken with Tomato Salsa.

Crisp Crumbed Chicken with Tomato Salsa

Preparation time:
  20 minutes
Total cooking time:
  40 minutes
Serves 6

1.25 kg chicken
  pieces
1 cup plain flour
1 tablespoon garlic
  pepper
2 egg whites, lightly
  beaten
2 cups cornflake
  crumbs

Tomato Salsa
1 medium tomato,
  finely chopped
1 small red onion,
  finely chopped
1 tablespoon chopped
  fresh coriander
1 tablespoon chopped
  fresh mint
2 tablespoons lemon
  juice
2 teaspoons finely
  grated lemon rind
1 teaspoon soft brown
  sugar

1 Preheat oven to moderate 180°C. Line an oven tray with foil. Trim chicken of excess fat and sinew. Remove skin. Combine flour and garlic pepper on sheet of greaseproof paper. Toss chicken lightly in seasoned flour; shake off excess.
2 Dip chicken pieces into egg whites a few pieces at a time. Coat with crumbs; shake off excess. Arrange pieces on prepared tray. Bake 40 minutes or until tender and coating crisp.
3 To make Salsa: Combine tomato, onion, coriander, mint, juice, rind and sugar in medium bowl. Cover with plastic wrap. Chill in refrigerator. Serve chicken with Tomato Salsa and crusty bread.

Beef Stroganoff.

Beef Stroganoff

Preparation time:
20 minutes
Total cooking time
20 minutes
Serves 6

500 g lean rump steak
1/2 cup cornflour
1 tablespoon sweet paprika
1 tablespoon sunflower oil
1 clove garlic, crushed
1 medium onion, sliced
100 g mushrooms, sliced
1 tablespoon Worcestershire sauce
440 g can peeled tomatoes, no added salt
1 tablespoon finely chopped parsley
250 g low-fat yoghurt

1 Trim meat of excess fat and cut into thin strips. Combine cornflour and paprika on sheet of greaseproof paper. Toss meat lightly in seasoned flour; shake off excess.
2 Heat oil in large non-stick frying pan. Add garlic and onion; cook over moderate heat for 2 minutes or until golden. Add meat in small batches; cook 5 minutes or until well browned. Return all meat to pan. Add mushrooms, Worcestershire sauce, tomatoes and parsley. Bring to boil; reduce heat. Simmer for 10 minutes.
3 Fold in yoghurt just before serving. Serve immediately with noodles and salad.

> **HINT**
> Use 500 g lean chicken breast fillet in place of beef in this recipe.

Family-style Lasagne

Preparation time:
  30 minutes
Total cooking time:
  40 minutes
Serves 6–8

1 large eggplant, sliced
18 sheets instant
  wholemeal lasagne
2 teaspoons
  polyunsaturated oil
1 clove garlic, crushed
1 large onion, chopped
1 red capsicum,
  chopped
500 g lean beef mince
800 g can peeled
  tomatoes, no added salt
2 tablespoons salt-
  reduced tomato paste
1 carrot, sliced
100 g mushrooms, sliced
2 zucchini, sliced
2 tablespoons finely
  chopped fresh basil
200 g low-fat ricotta
  cheese
200 g light mozzarella,
  grated

1 Preheat oven to
moderate 180°C.
Sprinkle eggplant with
salt; stand 20 minutes.
Rinse and pat dry with
paper towel.

*Clockwise from top
left: Spicy Bean
Casserole with
Cornmeal Topping
(page 36), Family-style
Lasagne, and Coq au
Vin (page 37).*

For Spicy Bean Casserole: Slice spring onions and fresh chilli; cook until soft.

Add pumpkin, zucchini, tomatoes, corn and kidney beans to pan.

2 Line base of deep oval ovenproof dish with lasagne sheets.
3 Heat oil in a large non-stick frying pan. Add garlic and onion and cook over medium heat for 2 minutes or until golden. Add capsicum and mince and cook 10 minutes or until well browned. Use a fork to break up mince lumps as it cooks. Drain off excess fat. Add tomatoes, tomato paste, carrot, mushrooms, zucchini and basil; stir until well combined. Bring mixture to boil. Reduce heat; simmer for 20 minutes.
4 Spoon meat mixture over lasagne, top with eggplant, one-third ricotta and mozzarella. Repeat layers with remaining ingredients. Bake 40 minutes or until lasagne is tender. Let stand 10 minutes. Serve with green salad and crusty bread.

Spicy Bean Casserole with Cornmeal Topping

Preparation time:
  25 minutes
Total cooking time:
  1 hour
Serves 6

2 teaspoons olive oil
onions
2 cloves garlic, crushed
4 spring onions, chopped
1 small red chilli, finely chopped
500 g pumpkin, cut into 3 cm cubes
3 zucchini, cut into large pieces
425 g can tomatoes, crushed
440 g can corn kernels, drained
440 g red kidney beans, drained

Dumplings
1 cup wholemeal self-raising flour
1 cup cornmeal (polenta)
3/4 cup low-fat milk
2 tablespoons finely chopped chives

1 Preheat oven to moderate 180°C.
2 Place oil in large pan. Add garlic, onions, chilli and cook over low heat until onions are soft. Add pumpkin, zucchini, undrained tomatoes, corn and kidney beans. Stir to combine. Transfer mixture to ovenproof dish. Cover and bake 45 minutes.
3 To make Dumplings: Sift flour into medium mixing bowl, add cornmeal and chives; mix. Make well in centre; add milk and mix with knife to a soft dough.
4 Remove bean mixture from oven and top with spoonsful of dumpling mixture. Return to oven uncovered. Bake another 15–20 minutes

For dumplings, make well in centre, add milk and mix to soft dough.

Top bean casserole with tablespoonfuls of dumpling mixture.

or until topping is cooked and golden brown.

Note: If you prefer a soft dumpling, simply cover the dish after adding the dumplings and cook for the same length of time.

Coq au Vin

Preparation time:
  40 minutes
Total cooking time:
  1 hour
Serves 4

1 tablespoon olive oil
1.5 kg chicken, skin and fat removed, cut into serving-size pieces
12 pickling onions, peeled
250 g button mushrooms, stalks trimmed
2 cloves garlic, crushed
60 g lean turkey ham, finely chopped

1/2 cup red wine
1 1/2 cups fresh chicken stock
2 bay leaves
2 tablespoons cornflour extra 1/4 cup water
1/2 cup finely chopped parsley

1 Remove giblets and any large deposits of fat from the chicken. Heat oil in heavy-based pan; add chicken pieces. Cook over high heat 2 minutes to seal, turning once. Reduce heat and cook a further 3 minutes on each side. Remove from pan; drain on paper towel.
2 Add onions and mushrooms to pan; cook over medium heat until onions are brown. Remove and set aside.
3 Add garlic and turkey ham to pan; cook for 2 minutes. Add wine, stock and bay leaves and bring slowly to the boil. Reduce heat, simmer.
4 Return chicken to

pan. Cover; simmer for 35 minutes or until chicken is cooked. Remove chicken from pan and keep warm. Add blended cornflour and water to pan. Stir constantly until sauce boils and thickens. Return chicken, add onions and mushrooms and reheat. Discard bay leaves.
5 Place Coq au Vin onto serving plate and top with parsley. Serve with steamed new potatoes and snow peas.

Note. Purchased chicken pieces could be used in this recipe. Remove all fat and sinew before cooking. Turkey ham is made from turkey thigh, smoked and cured to look and taste like ham. It is available from delicatessens and supermarkets. If unavailable, use lean ham instead.

Burger with the Lot

Preparation time:
  20 minutes
Total cooking time:
  20 minutes
Serves 6

500 g lean minced beef
¹/2 cup wholemeal
  breadcrumbs
3 spring onions,
  chopped
1 tablespoon teriyaki
  marinade
¹/3 cup grated low-fat
  mozzarella
6 wholegrain rolls
6 lettuce leaves
2 tomatoes, sliced
185 g beetroot slices
185 g pineapple thins

Relish
1 small onion, chopped
2 ripe tomatoes,
  chopped
1 tablespoon soft
  brown sugar
1 tablespoon tarragon
  vinegar

1 Combine mince, breadcrumbs, onions, marinade and cheese in large bowl. Mix well. Shape mixture into six patties, using three tablespoonsful for each. Arrange on foil-lined tray. Cook under grill on high heat for 5 minutes; turn and cook other side further 5 minutes or until browned and tender.

Transfer to plate; keep warm.
2 Cut rolls in half horizontally. Place under hot grill 2–3 minutes or until lightly toasted. Top one half of each roll with beef patty. Place lettuce, tomato, beetroot and pineapple on top. Place remaining bun on top. Serve with Relish.
3 To make Relish: Combine all ingredients in medium pan. Cook over medium heat for 15 minutes or until liquid is absorbed. Cool before serving.

Beef and Vegetable Kebabs

Preparation time:
  30 minutes +
  overnight marinating
Total cooking time:
  12 minutes
Serves 6

600 g rump steak
¹/4 cup salt-reduced
  soy sauce
¹/3 cup red wine
  vinegar
1 clove garlic,
  crushed
1 tablespoon grated
  green ginger
2 onions, cut into
  quarters

1 large red capsicum,
  seeded and cut into
  large cubes
¹/2 small fresh
  pineapple, peeled and
  cut into chunks

1 Trim meat of excess fat and sinew. Cut into 2.5 cm cubes. Combine soy, vinegar, garlic and ginger in large bowl. Add meat and stir to combine. Store, covered with plastic wrap, in refrigerator several hours or overnight. Drain and reserve marinade.
2 Thread meat, onions, capsicum and pineapple alternately onto skewers.
3 Place kebabs on cold grilling tray. Cook under medium heat for 12 minutes or until meat is tender, brushing with reserved marinade several times during cooking.
4 Serve kebabs accompanied by a crisp mixed leaf salad and boiled rice.

Note: Vegetables must be cut slightly thicker than the meat so they don't overcook.
A lean cut of pork could be used instead of the rump steak in this recipe.

Burger with the Lot (top) and Beef and Vegetable Kebabs.

Spaghetti and Meatballs

Preparation time:
 45 minutes
Total cooking time:
 40 minutes
Serves 6

1 clove garlic, crushed
1 onion, chopped
1 large carrot,
 chopped
1 kg ripe tomatoes,
 skinned and
 chopped
3 tablespoons
 tomato paste, no
 added salt
1/4 cup white wine
1/4 cup chicken
 stock
500 g lean minced veal
2 tablespoons cornflour
1 egg white
1/2 cup finely chopped
 basil leaves
500 g spaghetti

1 To make sauce: Place garlic, onion and carrot in non-stick medium pan. Cook over low heat until onion is soft. Add tomatoes, paste, wine and stock; bring slowly to the boil. Reduce heat, cover and simmer for 15 minutes. Remove from heat and cool slightly. Purée mixture in blender or food processor. Return to pan.
2 To make meatballs: Place veal, cornflour, egg white and basil in medium mixing bowl. Mix well, using wetted hand. Roll mixture into walnut-sized balls. Place balls into simmering sauce; cover and cook for 15 minutes.
3 To cook pasta: Place spaghetti in large pan of boiling water and cook until just tender. Drain.
4 Place pasta on serving plate; top with meatballs and sauce and garnish with fresh basil leaves.

Note: White or wholemeal spaghetti or any shape pasta can be used for this recipe. If desired, a little freshly grated parmesan cheese may be sprinkled on top just before serving.

Family Pizza

Preparation time:
 45 minutes +
 1 hour standing
Total cooking time:
 45 minutes
Makes one 30 cm pizza

Crust
1 tablespoon dried
 yeast
2/3 cup lukewarm
 water
1 cup wholemeal flour
1 cup plain flour
1 teaspoon dried
 oregano
1 teaspoon olive oil, to
 grease pan

Topping
1 clove garlic, crushed
3 tablespoons tomato
 paste, no added salt
1 onion, finely
 chopped
400 g can tomatoes, no
 added salt
2 teaspoons dried
 oregano
125 g lean minced beef
1 small green capsicum,
 finely chopped
100 g mushrooms,
 sliced
60 g low-fat mozzarella
 cheese, grated
8 black pitted olives,
 sliced

1 Preheat oven to hot 210°C (190°C gas). Brush 30 cm pizza pan with olive oil.
2 Combine yeast and water in small bowl; leave in warm position for 10 to 15 minutes or until bubbles appear.
3 Sift flours into bowl, returning bran husks to bowl. Add oregano and stir to combine. Make well in centre; add water and yeast mixture. Using a knife, mix to firm dough.
4 Turn dough onto lightly floured surface and knead for 5 minutes or until dough is smooth. Shape dough into ball; place into large lightly oiled bowl. Let stand covered with plastic wrap in

Family Pizza (left) and Spaghetti and Meatballs.

warm place for 1 hour or until well risen.

5 To prepare Topping: Place tomato paste, garlic and onion in small pan and cook over low heat until onion is soft. Add undrained tomatoes and oregano; cook uncovered over low heat until mixture has thickened. Remove from heat. Cool. Heat non-stick pan. Add mince and cook over medium heat 5 minutes or until well browned and all liquid has evaporated. Use a fork to break up any lumps whilst cooking. Remove from heat. Allow to cool.

6 Punch dough down, using fist. Turn onto lightly floured surface. Knead well for 3 minutes. Roll out to a 30 cm round. Place onto pizza tray.

7 Spread over tomato sauce. Top with beef, capsicum, mushrooms, cheese and olives.Bake for 25 to 30 minutes. Serve hot or cold, cut into wedges. Serve with salad.

41

Pork and Fruit Casserole

Preparation time:
  20 minutes
Total cooking time:
  1 hour
Serves 6–8

⅓ *cup plain flour*
750 g diced pork
4 medium green apples,
  peeled and cut into
  eighths
200 g dried apricots
200 g prunes, stones
  removed
1 cup apple juice
2 teaspoons seeded
  mustard
2 tablespoons lemon
  juice

1 Preheat oven to
moderate 180°C.
2 Place flour into a
large plastic bag. Add
prepared meat; secure
bag and shake,
ensuring all meat is
evenly coated with
flour. Shake off excess.

HINT
Dried apples may be
used in place of
fresh. Add an extra
¼ cup apple juice.
Any new- fashioned
cut of pork can be
used for this recipe
as long as it is
totally fat-free.

Pork and Fruit Casserole (top) and
Vegetable Risotto.

3 Place meat and fruit
in layers in ovenproof
dish, ending with a
layer of fruit.
4 Combine apple juice,
mustard and lemon
juice in jug. Pour over
meat and fruit. Cover,
bake for 1 hour. Serve
accompanied by pasta
and crisp green salad.

Vegetable Risotto

Preparation time:
  35 minutes
Total cooking time:
  45 minutes
Serves 4

1 teaspoon olive oil
1 large onion,
  chopped
1¼ cups short-grain
  rice
¼ cup dry white wine
4 to 5 cups hot chicken
  stock (see page 24)
½ cup frozen peas
½ cup frozen corn
  niblets

100 g button
  mushrooms, cut in
  half
2 large tomatoes,
  peeled, seeded and
  chopped
½ teaspoon freshly
  ground black pepper
1 teaspoon grated
  lemon rind
1 tablespoon lemon
  juice
30 g grated parmesan
  cheese

1 Heat oil in medium
pan. Add onion; stir
over medium heat until
golden; add rice.
2 Reduce heat to low;
stir rice 3 minutes or
until lightly golden.
Add wine and quarter
of the stock to the pan.
Stir continuously for
6 minutes or until
liquid is absorbed.
3 Repeat process,
stirring continuously,
until all liquid has been
added and rice is
almost tender. Add
vegetables; stir to
combine. Cover and
cook for 5 minutes.
4 Remove from heat.
Stand, covered,
3 minutes. Stir in
pepper, rind, lemon
juice, cheese and
parsley. Serve
immediately.

Note: Rice requires
constant stirring to
prevent burning and
sticking to base of the
pan. It is best to use a
heavy-based pan.

Oven-roasted Potatoes

Preparation time:
  25 minutes
Total cooking time:
  1 hour 45 minutes
Serves 6

*8 (200 g) washed
potatoes*

Filling 1
*225 g can red salmon,
  drained and flaked*
*1/2 cup low-fat cottage
  cheese*
*1/2 bunch chives,
  chopped*
2 teaspoons lemon juice
*1 teaspoon finely grated
  lemon rind*
*1/4 teaspoon freshly
  ground black pepper*

Filling 2
1 cup corn kernels
*1 medium red
  capsicum, seeded,
  chopped*
1 stick celery, chopped
*1/2 cup low-fat plain
  yoghurt*
*1 teaspoon seeded
  mustard*

1 Preheat oven to
moderate 180°C.
2 Place potatoes on
oven tray. Prick with a
skewer and cook for
1–1 1/2 hours, or until
golden brown and
tender.
3 To prepare fillings:
Place salmon, cottage
cheese, chives, lemon
juice, rind and pepper
into medium mixing
bowl. Stir to combine.
Place corn, capsicum,
celery, yoghurt and
mustard into mixing
bowl. Stir to combine.
4 Remove potatoes
from oven. Cut a lid
from each potato.
Carefully scoop out
contents. Place in
medium mixing bowl;
mash until smooth and
creamy. Set shells aside.
5 Divide mashed potato
in half; add to each
filling. Mix gently to
combine. Pile mixture
back into potato shells,
replace lids and bake
for 15 minutes more.
Serve hot, accompanied
by a tossed salad.

Paella

Preparation time:
  40 minutes
Total cooking time:
  40 minutes
Serves 6

3 chicken thigh fillets
*3 medium tomatoes,
  peeled and chopped*
125 g marinara mix
*1/2 large green
  capsicum, chopped*
*1/2 large red capsicum,
  chopped*
1 teaspoon olive oil
2 cloves garlic, crushed
*1 large red onion,
  chopped*
2 cups long-grain rice
*1/2 teaspoon ground
  turmeric*
4 cups chicken stock
*400 g canned artichoke
  hearts, drained*
*2 tablespoons chopped
  parsley*

1 Trim chicken of
excess fat and sinew.
Cut each thigh into
four pieces. Place
tomatoes in medium
pan; cook over low
heat 3 minutes. Add
chicken, marinara mix
and capsicum. Bring to
boil. Reduce heat and
simmer, uncovered,
5 minutes or until
chicken is cooked.
Remove and set aside.
2 Heat oil in large pan.
Add garlic and onion
and cook over medium
heat 1 minute or until
golden. Add rice and
stir well, making sure
rice grains are coated
with oil. Stir in turmeric
and stock; cover pan
with tight-fitting lid.
3 Bring stock slowly to
the boil; stir once.
Reduce heat; simmer
covered 20 minutes.
Add chicken mixture,
artichoke hearts and
parsley. Cover; cook
over low heat 5 minutes.
4 Remove from heat.
Let stand, covered,
5 minutes or until all
liquid is absorbed and
rice is tender. Separate
rice grains with a fork.

Oven-roasted Potatoes (top) and Paella.

Desserts

For the sweet tooth, there are plenty of satisfying and healthy alternatives to fresh seasonal fruit. Yoghurt substitutes for cream; ricotta cheese is used in cheesecake and pastry and as a filling for crêpes. Skim milk and other low-fat products are also invaluable for the health-conscious.

Banana and Apple Cake

Preparation time:
  20 minutes
Total cooking time:
  50 minutes
Serves 6

2 *cups self-raising flour*
2 *teaspoons baking powder*
1 *teaspoon ground cinnamon*
70 g *polyunsaturated margarine, melted*
1 *tablespoon honey*
1/2 *cup skim milk*
2 *eggs, lightly beaten*
3 *ripe bananas, mashed*
2 *apples, peeled, cored and chopped*

1 Preheat oven to moderate 180°C. Brush a 20 cm baba tin with melted margarine. Sift flour and remaining dry ingredients into a large mixing bowl. Make a well in the centre.
2 Combine margarine and honey in small pan. Stir over low heat until margarine has melted and mixture is smooth.
3 Add margarine mixture and combined milk and eggs gradually to dry ingredients. Stir until well combined and mixture is smooth. Stir in bananas and apple.
4 Pour mixture into prepared tin. Smooth surface. Bake for 50 minutes or until skewer comes out clean when inserted into centre of cake. Stand cake in tin 10 minutes before turning onto wire rack to cool. Serve cake plain or with a light dusting of icing sugar.

Banana and Apple Cake (right) and Lemon Meringue Pie (page 48).

Lemon Meringue Pie

Preparation time:
  30 minutes
Total cooking time:
  30 minutes
Serves 6–8

Pastry
2 cups plain flour
80 g polyunsaturated
  margarine
1 egg yolk
1 tablespoon lemon
  juice
2–3 tablespoons water

Filling
1/4 cup cornflour
1 1/4 cups water
1 teaspoon grated
  lemon rind
1/3 cup lemon
  juice
1 tablespoon honey
1 egg yolk

Meringue
2 egg whites
2 tablespoons honey

1 Preheat oven to
moderate 180°C. Brush
a 20 cm round pie dish
with melted margarine.
Place flour and
margarine in food
processor bowl. Using
pulse action, press for
10 seconds or until
mixture is fine and
crumbly. Add egg yolk
and almost all the
liquid, process for
15 seconds or until

mixture comes together.
Leave, covered with
plastic wrap, in
refrigerator for
20 minutes.
2 Roll pastry between
two sheets of plastic
wrap, large enough to
cover base and sides of
prepared dish. Cut a
sheet of greaseproof
paper large enough to
cover pastry-lined pie
dish. Spread a layer of
dried beans or rice
evenly over paper. Bake
for 10 minutes. Remove
from oven; discard
paper and beans/rice.
Return pastry to oven
for further 10 minutes
or until lightly golden.
Reduce heat to
moderately slow 160°C.
3 To make Filling:
Combine cornflour,
water, rind, juice and
honey in medium pan.
Stir constantly over
medium heat for
3 minutes or until
mixture boils and
thickens; boil 2 minutes
more. Remove from
heat; cool slightly. Add
egg yolk and beat well.
4 To make Meringue:
Place honey in small
pan. Bring to boil;
reduce heat and simmer
1 minute. Place egg
whites in small dry
mixing bowl. Using
electric beaters, beat
egg whites until soft
peaks form. Add honey
gradually, beating
constantly until mixture
is thick and glossy.

5 Spread filling evenly
over pastry base.
Spread or pipe
meringue decoratively
over the top. Bake
15 minutes or until
meringue is golden.
Stand pie on wire rack
to cool. Serve cold, cut
into wedges.

Note: To make orange
meringue pie, replace
lemon juice with orange
juice.

Caramel Soufflé

Preparation time:
  20 minutes
Total cooking time:
  15 minutes
*Makes four 3/4 cup
soufflés*

30 g polyunsaturated
  margarine
2 tablespoons soft
  brown sugar
1 tablespoon low-fat
  milk
2 tablespoons plain
  flour
2 eggs, separated
2 egg whites
1 teaspoon icing sugar

1 Preheat oven to
moderately slow 160°C.
Brush four 3/4 cup
capacity soufflé dishes
with melted margarine.
Heat margarine in
medium pan; add sugar.
Stir over low heat until
margarine has melted
and sugar dissolved.

Caramel Soufflé.

2 Add flour, stir over low heat 2 minutes or until flour mixture is golden. Add milk gradually to pan, stirring until mixture boils and thickens. Boil further 1 minute; remove from heat. Add egg yolks and beat until smooth. Transfer mixture to medium bowl.
3 Using electric beaters, beat egg whites in small dry mixing bowl until stiff peaks form. Using a metal spoon, fold gently into sugar mixture.
4 Spoon into prepared dishes; place on oven tray. Bake 15 minutes or until well risen and browned. Dust lightly with sifted icing sugar. Serve immediately.

Miniature Fruit Flans

Preparation time:
  30 minutes
Total cooking time:
  20 minutes
Serves 6

2 cups plain
  flour
80 g polyunsaturated
  margarine
1 egg yolk
1 tablespoon lemon
  juice
2–3 tablespoons iced
  water

Filling
2 tablespoons custard
  powder
1 tablespoon honey
1 1/4 cups skim milk

Topping
4 kiwi fruit, sliced
1/2 punnet strawberries,
  sliced

1 Preheat oven to
moderate 180°C. Brush
six 10 x 2 cm flan tins
with melted margarine.
Place flour and
margarine in food
processor bowl. Using
pulse action, press
button for 10 seconds
until mixture is fine
and crumbly. Add yolk,
lemon juice and almost
all the liquid. Process
20 seconds or until
mixture comes together.
Turn onto a lightly
floured surface and
knead 5 minutes. Stand
dough, covered with
plastic wrap, in
refrigerator 20 minutes.
2 Divide pastry into
six equal portions. Roll
pastry between two
sheets of plastic wrap,
large enough to cover
base and sides of
prepared tins.
3 Cut six sheets of
greaseproof paper large
enough to cover each
pastry-lined tin. Spread
a layer of dried beans
or rice evenly over
paper. Bake 10 minutes.
Remove from oven,
discard paper and rice.
Return pastry to oven
for a further
5 minutes or until
lightly golden. Cool.
4 To make Filling:
Combine custard
powder, honey and
milk in medium
saucepan. Stir over
medium heat until
mixture boils and
thickens. Cool.
5 Spoon custard
mixture into flan cases,
top with fruit. Serve.

> **HINT**
> Use slices of banana
> or mandarin to
> replace the
> strawberries and
> kiwi fruit if these
> are not in season.

Apricot Strudel

Preparation time:
  20 minutes
Total cooking time:
  40 minutes
Serves 6

4 sheets filo pastry
30 g polyunsaturated
  margarine, melted
1/4 cup ground almonds
800 g can apricot
  halves in natural juice,
  drained
100 g ricotta cheese
1/4 teaspoon ground
  cinnamon
1 tablespoon skim milk

1 Preheat oven to
moderate 180°C. Line
an oven tray with
baking paper. Lay one
sheet of pastry on top
of another. Brush top
with margarine,
sprinkle with almonds.
2 Place remaining two
sheets on top. Cover
with damp tea-towel to
prevent drying out.
3 Combine apricots,
ricotta and cinnamon
in a bowl. Mix well.
Place filling along one
edge of pastry, leaving
2 cm at each side. Fold
in sides and roll. Place
on prepared tray. Brush
with skim milk. Bake
for 40 minutes or until
golden. Serve strudel
hot with yoghurt or
low-fat ice-cream.

Apricot Strudel (top) and Miniature Fruit Flans.

For Fruit Puffs: Add flour all at once to water and margarine mixture.

Stir until mixture thickens and comes away from side of the pan.

Fruit Puffs

Preparation time:
50 minutes
Total cooking time:
40 minutes
*Makes 12 large
puffs*

³/4 cup water
50 g low-salt
   polyunsaturated
   margarine
³/4 cup plain flour
3 eggs, lightly beaten

Filling
300 g ricotta cheese
1 teaspoon vanilla
   essence
1 teaspoon icing
   sugar
125 g strawberries
   chopped
1 teaspoon icing sugar,
   extra

1 Preheat oven to
moderately hot 210°C
(190°C gas). Brush a
large baking tray
with oil.
2 Combine water and
margarine in a medium
pan. Stir over low heat
until margarine has
melted. Bring quickly to
the boil. Remove pan
from heat and add
flour all at once.
Using a wooden spoon,
beat until mixture is
smooth.
3 Return to medium
heat and continue to
stir until the mixture
thickens and comes
away from the side and
base of the pan.
4 Remove from heat
and cool slightly.
Transfer mixture to
small bowl of electric
mixer. Using electric
beaters, add beaten
eggs gradually, beating
until mixture is glossy
and firm.
5 Sprinkle tray with
water. Place spoonfuls
of mixture on tray.
Sprinkle again with

water. Bake for 8 to
10 minutes or until
puffs are well risen and
golden brown. Reduce
heat to 180°C and cook
for a further 20 minutes
or until golden brown
and crisp.
6 Cool puffs in oven
with door ajar for
15 minutes. Remove
from oven. Cut each
puff in half and, using
teaspoon, remove any
uncooked mixture.
Reduce heat to
moderately slow
160°C oven. Bake for
5 minutes or until
puffs are crisp and dry.
Remove from oven.
Cool on wire rack.
7 To make Filling:
Using electric beaters,
beat ricotta cheese,
essence and icing sugar
until thick and creamy.
Fold in strawberries.
Place a spoonful of
filling in the base of
each puff; top with lid.
Sift over extra icing
sugar and serve the
puffs immediately.

Fruit Puffs.

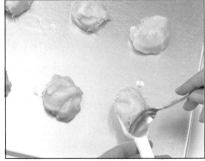

*Sprinkle tray with water; place spoonfuls
of mixture on it and sprinkle again.*

*Fold the strawberries into the ricotta
and icing sugar mixture.*

53

Crêpes with Tangy Orange Sauce

Preparation time:
  10 minutes
Total cooking time:
  15 minutes
Serves 4

2 cups plain flour
2 eggs, lightly
  beaten
2 cups skim milk
1/2 teaspoon almond
  essence
1 teaspoon finely
  grated orange rind

Sauce
*juice and rind of
  4 oranges
2 tablespoons lemon
  marmalade
2 tablespoons Grand
  Marnier*

1 Place all crêpe
ingredients in food
processor bowl or
blender.
2 Using pulse action,
press button for
15 seconds or until
ingredients are
combined and mixture
is free of lumps.
Transfer mixture to jug.
Leave to stand, covered
with plastic wrap, for
10 minutes.
3 Pour 2-3 tablespoons
batter onto 20 cm non-
stick crêpe pan. Cook
over medium heat
2 minutes or until
underside is golden.

Turn crêpe over, cook
other side. Transfer to
plate; cover with tea-
towel, keep warm.
4 To make Orange
Sauce: Place all
ingredients in non-stick
frying pan and stir over
medium heat. Bring to
boil; reduce heat and
simmer 10 minutes.
Fold crêpes in quarters;
add to pan in batches.
Serve crêpes warm with
yoghurt or ricotta
cheese.

Note: For a great filling
idea: Mix 100 g ricotta
cheese with 1/4 teaspoon
ground cinnamon and
1/4 teaspoon ground
cloves. Place two
teaspoons of mixture
inside each crêpe. Pour
sauce over to serve.

Baked Cheesecake

Preparation time:
  20 minutes
Total cooking time:
  1 hour
Serves 6–8

*250 g shredded
  wheatmeal biscuits,
  crushed
20 g polyunsaturated
  margarine, melted
1 egg white, lightly
  beaten*

Filling
*300 g silken tofu
250 g low-fat ricotta
  cheese
1 egg, lightly beaten
1/4 cup honey
1 tablespoon lemon
  juice
1 tablespoon finely
  grated lemon rind*

1 Preheat oven to
moderately slow
160°C. Line base of
20 cm round
springform tin with
greaseproof paper.
Combine biscuits,
margarine and egg
white in a medium
bowl. Mix well. Press
mixture firmly into
base and halfway up
sides of tin.
2 To make Filling:
Place tofu, ricotta
cheese, egg, honey, juice
and rind into food
processor bowl. Using
pulse action, press
button for 15 seconds
or until mixture is
smooth.
3 Pour mixture onto
biscuit base. Bake for
1 hour or until set.
Remove from oven;
cool. Cut into wedges
to serve.

HINT
Decorate the Baked
Cheesecake with
segments of peeled
orange, if liked.

---

*Baked Cheesecake (top) and Crêpes with Tangy
Orange Sauce.*

Orange and Passionfruit Mousse

Preparation time:
  1 hour + 1 hour
  refrigeration
Total cooking time:
  3–4 minutes
Serves 4–6

1 tablespoon gelatine
1/2 cup cold water
2 tablespoons plain
  flour
1/4 cup honey
1 cup orange juice
1 tablespoon lemon
  juice
1/2 cup hot water
1/2 cup passionfruit pulp

1 Sprinkle gelatine over cold water; set aside.
2 Combine flour and honey in small pan; add small amount of orange juice to blend to a smooth paste.
3 Add remaining orange juice, lemon juice and hot water. Stir constantly over medium heat until mixture boils and thickens. Remove from heat.
4 Add soaked gelatine; stir until dissolved. Pour mixture into a metal tray and refrigerate until just beginning to set.

5 Transfer mixture to large bowl of electric mixer and beat until mixture is light, airy and doubled in volume.
6 Fold in passionfruit pulp. Place mixture into one large or individual serving dishes. Refrigerate for 1 to 2 hours before serving.

Apple Pie

Preparation time:
  1 hour
Total cooking time:
  45 minutes
Makes one 20 cm pie

Pastry
3/4 cup wholemeal flour
3/4 cup plain flour
60 g ricotta cheese
30 g polyunsaturated
  margarine
1 tablespoon lemon
  juice
2–3 tablespoons cold
  water

Filling
6 large green apples,
  peeled, quartered and
  sliced
1 teaspoon grated
  lemon rind
1 tablespoon plain flour
1 teaspoon ground
  cinnamon
1 egg white
1/2 teaspoon ground
  cinnamon, extra

1 Preheat oven to moderate 180°C.
2 To prepare Pastry: Sift flours into large mixing bowl; return husks to bowl.
3 Combine ricotta and margarine, using a fork. Using fingertips, rub ricotta and butter into flour until mixture resembles fine breadcrumbs.
4 Add lemon juice and water to form a soft dough. Store, covered with plastic wrap, in refrigerator for 15 minutes.
5 Roll out two-thirds pastry on lightly floured surface until 5 mm thick or large enough to cover base and sides of 20 cm pie plate. Using a sharp knife, trim off excess.
6 To prepare Filling: Toss apples in combined flour, cinnamon and lemon rind. Place evenly in pie dish.
7 Roll out remaining pastry and cut into thin strips. Place on top to form a lattice pattern.
8 Brush lattice top with lightly beaten egg white and sprinkle with cinnamon.
9 Bake for 45 minutes or until apple is tender and pastry golden brown.

Note: Serve pie with spoonfuls of whipped, vanilla-flavoured ricotta cheese.

Apple Pie (left) and Orange and Passionfruit Mousse.

57

Pavlova Yoghurt Roll

Preparation time:
  30 minutes +
  30 minutes
  refrigeration
Total cooking time:
  15 minutes
Serves 4–6

4 egg whites
1/2 cup caster sugar
1 teaspoon cornflour
1 teaspoon white vinegar
2 teaspoons icing sugar

Filling
1 cup low-fat plain
  yoghurt
250 g ricotta cheese
1/4 cup fresh
  passionfruit pulp
125 g punnet
  strawberries, sliced

1 Preheat oven to moderate 180°C. Brush 30 x 25 x 2 cm Swiss roll tin with melted margarine. Line base with paper; grease paper. Dust with sifted cornflour, shake off excess.

2 Place egg whites in small dry mixing bowl. Using electric beaters, beat egg whites until firm peaks form. Add sugar gradually, beating constantly until mixture is thick and glossy and all the sugar is dissolved.

3 Using a metal spoon, fold in cornflour and vinegar. Spread mixture into prepared tray. Bake for 12 to 15 minutes or until well risen and golden brown.

4 Turn meringue onto a sheet of greaseproof paper that has been lightly dusted with icing sugar. Leave to cool to lukewarm.

5 To make Filling: Using electric beaters, beat yoghurt and ricotta cheese until creamy. Cover and refrigerate 30 minutes before using. Spread Filling evenly over cooled meringue and top with fruit. Using paper as guide, roll from short side as for a Swiss roll. Cut in thick slices to serve.

Note: Meringue roll can be made a day ahead. Cover loosely with plastic wrap in refrigerator. Chill filling well before using. Meringue needs to be lukewarm for rolling, or it will crack.

Pavlova Yoghurt Roll.

For Pavlova Yoghurt Roll: Beat egg whites, adding sugar gradually.

Spread meringue mixture onto prepared tray; bake until golden brown.

Turn cooked meringue onto a sheet of greaseproof paper; leave to cool.

Spread filling over meringue and roll from short side, as for a Swiss roll.

Baked Rice Custard

Preparation time:
  20 minutes
Total cooking time:
  1 hour 5 minutes
Serves: 4–6

¹/4 cup short-grain rice
2 eggs, lightly beaten
¹/3 cup maple syrup
1¹/4 cups light
  evaporated milk
¹/2 cup water
¹/4 cup sultanas
¹/4 teaspoon ground
  cinnamon

1 Preheat oven to moderately slow 160°C.
2 Cook rice in medium pan of boiling water until just tender, drain.
3 Whisk together eggs, syrup, milk and water. Stir in rice and sultanas.
4 Pour mixture into deep 20 cm round or square ovenproof dish.
5 Place dish into a deep baking dish. Pour in enough hot water to come halfway up the sides. Bake 30 minutes. Sprinkle with cinnamon and bake 20 minutes more or until custard is set and a sharp knife comes out clean when inserted in centre. Remove from water immediately. Serve hot.

Macerated Strawberries with Yoghurt Maple Cream

Preparation time:
  10 minutes
Total cooking time:
  Nil
Serves 4

¹/3 cup low-joule
  raspberry cordial
1 cup water
1 tablespoon
  brandy
2 x 250 g punnets
  strawberries, cut in
  half

Maple Cream
1 cup low-fat
  yoghurt
1 tablespoon maple
  syrup
¹/4 cup pecans,
  chopped

1 Combine cordial, water and brandy in a medium bowl.
2 Add strawberries to mixture and stir until combined. Cover and refrigerate for 2 hours.
3 To make Maple Cream: Combine yoghurt, syrup and pecans. Mix well.
4 Serve strawberries with Maple Cream.

Baked Rice Custard (left) and Macerated Strawberries with Yoghurt Maple Cream.

Super Choc-liqueur Sandwich

Preparation time:
  1 hour
Total cooking time:
  25 minutes
Makes one 20 cm cake

2 eggs
2 egg whites
1/2 cup caster sugar
2/3 cup self-raising flour
2 tablespoons cocoa
  powder
1 tablespoon hot water
2 tablespoons
  chocolate-flavoured
  liqueur
100 g dried apricots,
  chopped
1/2 cup water
250 g ricotta cheese
1 teaspoon icing sugar
1 teaspoon icing sugar,
  extra
1 teaspoon cocoa
  powder

1 Preheat oven to moderate 180°C. Brush two 18 cm sandwich tins with melted margarine. Line base and sides with baking paper.
2 Using electric beaters, beat eggs and whites in small mixing bowl for 8 minutes or until thick and pale. Add sugar gradually, beating constantly until mixture is pale yellow and glossy. Transfer to a large mixing bowl.

3 Using a metal spoon, fold in sifted flour and cocoa with hot water and liqueur quickly and lightly. Spread mixture evenly into prepared tins. Bake 25 minutes or until sponges are lightly golden and shrink away from side of tins. Stand in tins 5 minutes before turning onto wire rack to cool.
4 Combine apricots and water in small pan. Cover and cook over low heat until apricots are tender and water has evaporated. Remove from heat. Beat with a wooden spoon to form a paste. Allow to cool.
5 Using electric beaters, beat ricotta and icing sugar until thick and creamy. To assemble cake: Place first layer on a board. Spread with apricot paste. Top with half ricotta cheese. Place remaining cake on top.
6 Transfer to serving plate and top with remaining ricotta cheese mixture. Dust with combined icing sugar and cocoa.

Note: Cooked, cooled, unfilled sponge can be frozen for one month, wrapped in plastic or in an airtight container.

Frozen Soft-serve Yoghurt

Preparation time:
  35 minutes +
  4 hours freezing
Total cooking time:
  Nil
Serves 4–6

1 tablespoon gelatine
2 tablespoons water
300 ml reduced-fat
  plain yoghurt
1 1/2 cups peach purée
2 tablespoons honey
2 teaspoons lemon juice

1 Combine gelatine with water in a small bowl. Stand in boiling water; stir until dissolved.
2 Place yoghurt, purée, honey, lemon juice and gelatine into food processor bowl. Using pulse action, process 20 seconds.
3 Transfer mixture into shallow metal tray. Cover and freeze for 2 hours. Return mixture to processor bowl. Using pulse action, process for 3 minutes. Return mixture to metal tray; freeze 2 hours more.
4 Return mixture to food processor bowl. Using pulse action, process for 3 minutes. Serve immediately.

Super Choc-liqueur Sandwich (top) and Frozen Soft-serve Yoghurt.

Index

*Page numbers in italics
refer to pictures*

Apple Pie 56, 57
Apricot Strudel 50, 51

Banana and Apple Cake
    46, 47
Bean Casserole, Spicy,
    with Cornmeal
    Topping 34, 36
Beef and Bean
    Burritos 26, 27
Beef and Vegetable
    Kebabs 38, 39
Beef Curry 16, 17
Beef Stir-fry 24, 25
Beef Stroganoff 33, 33
Burger with the
    Lot 38, 39

Caramel Soufflé 48, 49
Carrot and Poppyseed
    Salad 20, 21
Cheesecake,
    Baked, 54, 55
Chicken Kebabs,
    Spicy, 4, 5
Choc-liqueur Sandwich,
    Super, 62, 63
Cinnamon Pears with
    Vanilla Cream 20, 21
Coleslaw, Tangy, 4, 5
Coq au Vin 34, 37
Corn Muffins 7, 7
Crêpes with Tangy
    Orange Sauce 54, 55
Crisp Crumbed Chicken
    with Tomato Salsa
    32, 32
Cucumber and Melon
    Salad 18, 19
Eggplant Dip 2, 3

Family Pizza 40, 41
Family-style
    Lasagne 34, 35
Fish and Chips 30, 31
Frozen Peach Ice 8, 9
Frozen Soft-serve
    Yoghurt 62, 63
Fruit Flans,
    Miniature, 50, 51
Fruit Puffs 52, 53

Herb Roast
    Lamb 12, 13

Lemon Meringue
    Pie 47, 48

Mushroom Pâté 10, 11

Orange and Passionfruit
    Mousse 56, 57

Paella 44, 45
Pavlova Yoghurt
    Roll 58, 59
Potato and Onion
    Crisps 13, 13
Pork and Fruit
    Casserole 42, 43
Potatoes,
    Oven-roasted, 44, 45

Quiche Lorraine 26, 27

Ratatouille 12, 13
Red Lentil Dip 16, 17
Rice Custard,
    Baked, 60, 61
Roast Lamb with all the
    Trimmings 28, 29

Spaghetti and
    Meatballs 40, 41
Strawberries, Macerated,
    with Yoghurt Maple
    Cream 60, 61
Strawberry
    Mousse 14, 15
Sweet and Sour
    Chicken 22, 23
Sweet Potato
    Soup 11, 12

Tomato Salad 6, 6
Tuna Casserole 30, 31

Vegetable
    Frittatas 23, 24
Vegetables,
    Fragrant, 18, 19
Vegetable Risotto 42, 43
Vegie Burgers 3, 4